CORE LIBRARY GUIDE TO COVID-19

FLATTENING THE CURVE

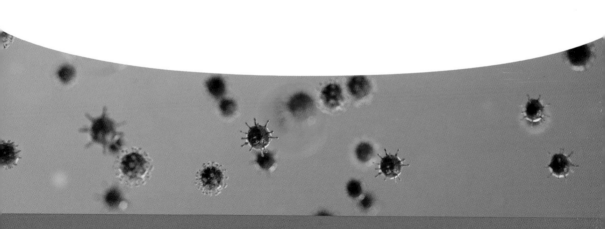

BY MARTHA LONDON

CONTENT CONSULTANT
Mark N. Lurie, PhD
Associate Professor of Epidemiology, International Health Institute
Brown University School of Public Health

Cover image: People wore face masks to help reduce the spread
of COVID-19.

Core Library

An Imprint of Abdo Publishing
abdobooks.com

abdobooks.com

Published by Abdo Publishing, a division of ABDO, PO Box 398166, Minneapolis, Minnesota 55439. Copyright © 2021 by Abdo Consulting Group, Inc. International copyrights reserved in all countries. No part of this book may be reproduced in any form without written permission from the publisher. Core Library™ is a trademark and logo of Abdo Publishing.

Printed in the United States of America, North Mankato, Minnesota
072020
092020

Cover Photo: Konstantin Zibert/Shutterstock Images
Interior Photos: Alex Potemkin/iStockphoto, 4–5; Ng Han Guan/AP Images, 7; Shutterstock Images, 8, 26–27, 45; Steven Senne/AP Images, 11; SDI Productions/iStockphoto, 14–15; iStockphoto, 17, 20 (cardboard), 20 (glass), 20 (plastic), 20 (stainless steel), 20 (wood), 29, 39, 43; Red Line Editorial, 20 (graph); Free Life Design/iStockphoto, 20 (copper); Syda Productions/Shutterstock Images, 22–23; Rich Pedroncelli/AP Images, 30; Eldar Nurkovic/Shutterstock Images, 34–35

Editor: Charly Haley
Series Designer: Jake Nordby

Library of Congress Control Number: 2020936514

Publisher's Cataloging-in-Publication Data

Names: London, Martha, author.
Title: Flattening the curve / by Martha London
Description: Minneapolis, Minnesota : Abdo Publishing, 2021 | Series: Core library guide to COVID-19 | Includes online resources and index
Identifiers: ISBN 9781532194047 (lib. bdg.) | ISBN 9781644945018 (pbk.) | ISBN 9781098212957 (ebook)
Subjects: LCSH: Communicable diseases--Prevention--Juvenile literature. | Distance education--Juvenile literature. | Social distance--Juvenile literature. | Hygiene--Juvenile literature. | Quarantine--Juvenile literature. | Epidemics--Juvenile literature. | COVID-19 (Disease)--Juvenile literature.
Classification: DDC 614.54--dc23

CONTENTS

SLOWING INFECTIONS

In March 2020, a new disease called COVID-19 was spreading across the United States and around the world. US governors began issuing shelter-in-place orders. People were asked to stay at home and not meet in groups. This could slow the spread of the disease. Businesses and parks closed. Schools closed too. Many kids had to finish the school year online.

Some parents in California got laptops from schools to help their children learn

Many children had to quickly switch from classes at school to distance learning at home because of the COVID-19 pandemic.

at home. But not all families were able to drive to schools to get the laptops. Others did not have internet access at home. Cecilia Madrid was the principal at Robert F. Kennedy School in Compton, California. She helped by bringing laptops to families' homes. If people did not have internet access, Madrid and the teachers printed learning packets. Madrid wanted to do everything she could to help her students succeed.

Like Madrid, teachers across the United States had to adjust for online learning. Schools closed to keep kids and families safe. It was not safe to gather in crowds during the pandemic. A sick person could infect many people in a crowd. Closing schools was one of many actions people took to help flatten the curve.

WHAT IS THE CURVE?

The COVID-19 pandemic began in China in late 2019. It soon spread to the rest of the world. Many news headlines used the phrase *flatten the curve*. The "curve" refers to a graph of the number of infections over time.

COVID-19 was first found in Wuhan, China. Officials tried many things to stop the disease from spreading, including using physical barriers to close off some parts of the city.

Viral infections such as COVID-19 start slowly with only a few people infected and then grow quickly as those people infect others. This is called an exponential rise. A lot of infections happen in a few months. With many diseases, people who recover have immunity from the virus. This means they will not get sick again. At a certain point, enough people have become ill and

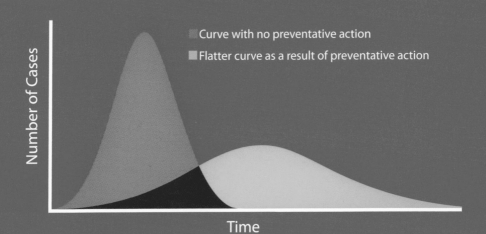

Curve with no preventative action
Flatter curve as a result of preventative action

Number of Cases

Time

This graph shows what flattening the curve could look like. How does this graph help you better understand the reasons why health officials wanted to flatten the curve during the COVID-19 pandemic?

recovered. The virus infects fewer and fewer people. This is when the curve on the graph begins to fall.

If nothing is done to slow the spread, the curve is a short, sharp peak. When infections are at their highest levels, there may not be enough hospital beds for all the sick people. Health-care systems get overwhelmed. Hospitals do not have enough equipment. Many people cannot get the care they need. Some people may die.

Flattening the curve means taking actions to slow the spread of a virus. The flatter curve shows infections spread out over a longer amount of time. The total number of infections may not change. But the peak is lower. Hospitals have more time to prepare. They have enough resources to care for people who get sick.

THE VIRUS

COVID-19 is caused by a virus called SARS-CoV-2. It is a type of virus called a coronavirus. This virus was first discovered in late 2019. Some people who get COVID-19 do not feel sick at all. Others have mild symptoms. They may run a fever and have a cough. But for some people, the symptoms are severe. These people develop respiratory infections. The virus attacks their lungs. They have trouble breathing. Some die from the disease.

Doctors and scientists studied the new coronavirus. They learned about how the virus spreads. The virus can be spread on objects. But scientists believe it mostly

PERSPECTIVES

WORKING TOGETHER

Ventilators are machines used to help hospital patients breathe. Before the pandemic, hospitals typically had some ventilators. But COVID-19 created a need for many more. States across the country requested ventilators from the federal government. But few states received the number they needed. As a result, some states loaned ventilators to one another. New York was hit especially hard. In early April, California governor Gavin Newsom sent 500 ventilators to New York and New Jersey. Newsom said, "I know that if the tables were turned and we were experiencing a hospital surge, other states would come to our aid and provide ventilators just as we are today."

spreads through the air between people. This is why people staying away from each other could help flatten the curve.

Infected people sneeze and cough. When they do, tiny droplets of spit or mucus enter the air. These droplets hold the virus. Droplets can even enter the air when people talk or breathe. Sometimes people inhale droplets with the virus. These people may become sick.

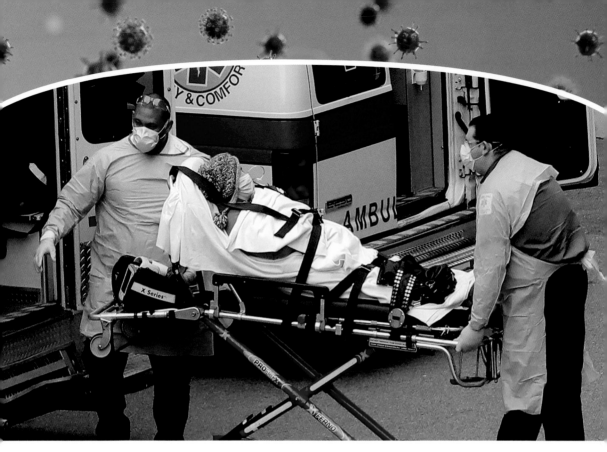

Hospitals around the world were overwhelmed by the high numbers of COVID-19 patients who needed treatment.

Masks were required in many public places. Masks can keep sick people from infecting others. There are several types of face masks. Doctors usually wear N95 masks. These masks are a type of respirator. They filter out most droplets in the air. Experts told people not to buy N95 masks. They wanted to make sure doctors had enough. Many people made their own cloth masks instead.

DIFFERENT FACE MASKS

In March 2020, the US Centers for Disease Control and Prevention (CDC) recommended all people wear some type of face covering in public. Due to shortages of N95 masks, the CDC recommended other options for the public. Some people chose to use surgical masks. These masks are thrown away after use. Other people chose to buy or make cloth masks. Cloth masks can be reused. They should be washed after each use. Scientists recommend washing masks in hot water and drying on high heat. Heat is more likely to kill viruses than cold water and air-drying. Cloth masks and surgical masks keep large droplets from getting into the air when people breathe or cough.

Flattening the curve took many forms. Some actions seemed small. By washing their hands regularly, people helped slow the spread of the virus. Other actions were more difficult. For example, people had to stay at home. They might have missed seeing friends or family. Some people lost their jobs when businesses closed. But flattening the curve gave hospitals a chance to prepare for COVID-19. The goal of this was to save lives.

STRAIGHT TO THE
SOURCE

Christian Lindmeier works for the World Health Organization. This organization tracked COVID-19 around the world. In an interview, Lindmeier explained how important it was to slow the rate of infections:

> We need to slow down the curve and slow down the spread and try to spread it over time as good as possible so that the health system can cope and production of vital medical equipment can cope. . . .
>
> One thing that is cutting transmission is . . . testing every single patient and following up on them. . . .
>
> The other is the various political measures, such as social distancing or quarantines.

Source: Sam Meredith. "Flattening the Coronavirus Curve." *CNBC*, cnbc.com, 19 Mar. 2020. Accessed 24 Apr. 2020

CONSIDER YOUR AUDIENCE

Review this passage closely. Consider how you would adapt it for a different audience, such as your parents or friends. Write a blog post conveying this same information for the new audience. What is the most effective way to get your point across? How does your new approach differ from the original text, and why?

WASH AND DISINFECT

Viruses such as SARS-CoV-2 travel out in droplets when a sick person breathes, coughs, or sneezes. Those droplets land on objects nearby. If people touch these objects, the droplets can get on their hands. Then if people touch their nose, eyes, or mouth, the virus can enter their bodies. Maintaining personal hygiene can help stop the virus from spreading this way. Washing hands and disinfecting surfaces keeps people safe.

COVID-19 is spread from person to person, including if one person coughs near another.

SOAP AND WATER

The US Centers for Disease Control and Prevention (CDC) says washing with soap and water is the best way to clean one's hands. It has guidelines for how to wash hands. People should wash their hands for at least 20 seconds using soap and running water. Each of these pieces is important.

Studies show that washing for 20 seconds removes enough dirt and germs to effectively prevent people from getting sick. The CDC reminds people to wash between fingers and even under the fingernails. People should also make sure to wash the backs of their hands. Washing for 20 seconds allows soap to remove or kill harmful germs, including viruses.

Soap is just as important as time. People do not need to use antibacterial soap. Any soap is better than water alone. Viruses such as the coronavirus have a protective layer of fats. Soap soaks up the fats. It breaks the outer layer of the virus. Soaps destroys the virus.

The simple act of washing hands was considered one of the most important steps to flattening the curve of COVID-19.

The last piece is running water. People do not need to leave the water running the whole time they wash their hands. But they should use running water to rinse at the end. Running water washes soap suds away more effectively than standing water. Standing water can also hold germs in it. It can make handwashing less effective.

HAND SANITIZER

People do not always have access to a sink with soap and water. Sometimes people need to disinfect when they are at a store. In these cases, the CDC recommends hand sanitizer. But not all hand sanitizer is the same. To kill the coronavirus, hand sanitizer has to have a certain alcohol content. The alcohol kills viruses and bacteria.

Most hand sanitizers contain alcohol. Others do not.

WET OR DRY?

Drying one's hands is just as important as washing them. According to the Mayo Clinic, wet hands spread germs more easily than dry hands. The CDC recommends using a clean towel or paper towel to completely dry hands after washing. Clean towels are important. Towels that have been reused may have germs on them. Those germs can come back into contact with a person when he or she uses the towel again.

They use a different chemical instead. This chemical stops or slows the growth of germs. But it does not kill them. The most effective hand sanitizers are at least 60 percent alcohol.

CLEANING SURFACES

Experts believe COVID-19 mostly spreads from person to person, either through the air or by direct contact between people. But the virus can also live on surfaces. Dirty surfaces can spread the virus to clean hands. It is important to clean surfaces that people touch often.

COVID-19 ON SURFACES

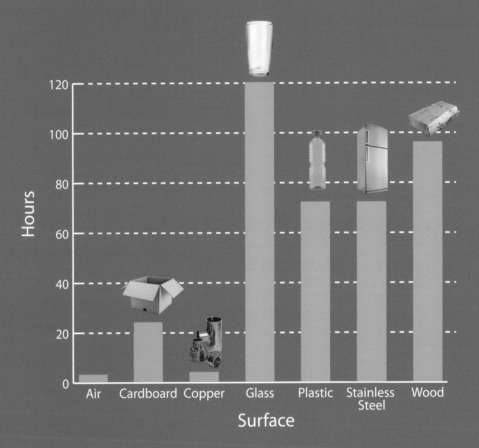

The graph above shows how long the coronavirus can survive on certain surfaces. How does the image help you understand how cleaning helped slow the spread of COVID-19?

These may include doorknobs, counters, phones, and remote controls.

The CDC recommends cleaning surfaces with soap and water, then disinfectant. As with handwashing, the soap and water remove dirt from surfaces. The disinfectant can kill remaining germs. People can buy disinfectant cleaners. They can also follow CDC guidelines to make their own by mixing bleach and water. It is important to allow bleach-based cleaners to air-dry. This allows the cleaner to completely kill viruses.

EXPLORE ONLINE

Chapter Two talks about the importance of handwashing to prevent illnesses. The article at the website below goes into more depth on this topic. Does the article answer any of the questions you had about hand hygiene?

THE SCIENCE OF HOW TO WASH YOUR HANDS

abdocorelibrary.com/flattening-the-curve

SOCIAL DISTANCING

Social distancing is purposefully limiting contact with other people. This includes limiting time in public spaces. When people used social distancing, they were less likely to get COVID-19. They came into contact with fewer people and objects.

As the pandemic continued, some organizations began to use the term *physical distancing* instead of *social distancing*. Social interactions are very important, and people can stay social while staying far apart. They do this

Many people started using video chats more often to stay in touch with friends and family while social distancing.

online or with phones. Distancing was an important step to flatten the curve.

HOW CLOSE IS TOO CLOSE?

States across the country urged people to stay inside as much as possible. Some states came up with illustrations to show the public how important social distancing was. For example, the Ohio Department of Health created a video using mousetraps and a ping-pong ball. The mousetraps were a symbol for people, and the ping-pong ball symbolized the coronavirus. It showed that when the mousetraps were close together, all of them snapped when the ball dropped because one mousetrap triggered another. But when the mousetraps were separated, none snapped. When people are separated, they are less likely to become infected.

People can spread the virus even if they do not show symptoms. The CDC recommended people stay at least 6 feet (1.8 m) apart. This distance is based on how far large droplets travel in the air before falling to the ground.

Scientists and researchers learned more about the virus as the pandemic continued. Later studies showed that tiny droplets could likely travel much farther than 6 feet. A sneeze causes droplets to travel farther because they leave a person's mouth at a higher speed. A breeze could carry tiny droplets more than 20 feet (6.1 m).

Still, the official recommendation was 6 feet. Researchers agreed that some distance was better than no distance. People could also take other precautions such as wearing a mask.

NEIGHBORHOOD DANCE PARTY

As people distanced from each other to slow the spread of COVID-19, many found new ways to have fun while staying safe. Some neighborhoods had distanced dance parties. In Buffalo, New York, one person played music from a balcony. Everyone on the street came out of their houses to dance. People stayed in their yards to keep a safe distance.

If people had to meet in person during the pandemic, they often wore masks and stayed 6 feet apart.

STAYING HOME

Shelter-in-place orders, also called stay-at-home orders, meant people spent more time at home with their families. Health organizations said being around immediate family or roommates was OK. What was important was limiting contact with strangers. Researchers did tell families to take extra precautions

for people who were elderly or who had existing health conditions. These people may have weaker immune systems. If infected, they were more likely to have a difficult time fighting off COVID-19. Extra precautions could include disinfecting and washing hands and clothes more frequently. It could also mean limiting contact with that family member as much as possible.

It is not possible for most people to stay home all the time. People need to buy food. Some may need to get necessary medications. Health experts said people should limit those outings as much as possible during the pandemic. They recommended going to the store or pharmacy once a week or less if possible.

Some people chose to have groceries or meals delivered. Many food delivery apps started offering contactless delivery. Delivery drivers left food at the door instead of talking to customers. Drivers could stay safe this way too. They came into contact with fewer customers.

Additionally, experts suggested only one person from a family should go on necessary shopping trips. This would reduce the number of people coming into contact with each other at stores. Some stores created rules that allowed only one person per cart. People were also asked to wear masks at stores and

During the pandemic, more people began getting food delivered so they could stay home.

to stay at least 6 feet away from other shoppers.

Companies wanted people to stay healthy and safe.

HOW LONG?

Flattening the curve looked different in different places.

Government leaders made decisions they felt were

best for their citizens. The United States was only one

California's governor, Gavin Newsom, spoke at a fire station in May 2020 about the state's coronavirus response.

of the many countries around the world affected by the pandemic. Some countries were more successful at flattening the curve than others. For example, South Korea tested many people for COVID-19. Officials used information from testing to see where the disease had spread in the country. This helped them work to contain the outbreak and reduce South Korea's number of COVID-19 cases.

In the United States, each state had different rules. Some states flattened the curve more than others. These states were able to begin reopening some businesses sooner than other states.

For example, California's stay-at-home order began on March 19, 2020. California was one of the first states to have this rule. As a result, its COVID-19 case numbers stayed relatively low early in the pandemic. According to the Institute for Health Metrics and Evaluation, California reached a peak in cases in late April. After that, the number of new cases began to decline. With these encouraging signs, Governor Gavin Newsom began relaxing some rules.

Government leaders across the country had a lot to consider in deciding when and how to relax the rules. This included thinking about how to reopen businesses

PERSPECTIVES

HOW SOON IS TOO SOON?

Although President Donald Trump's administration issued social distancing recommendations for the United States, Trump said he did not want businesses and employees to suffer from being closed too long. Much of the United States had done a good job of flattening the curve. But health experts said if stay-at-home orders were lifted too soon, new outbreaks would occur. Scientists said easing rules should come slowly. Krutika Kuppalli studies diseases. In an interview, Kuppalli said, "Once things get better, we will have to take a step-wise approach toward letting up on these measures and see how things go to prevent things from getting worse again."

and schools. Some people were concerned that opening up too fast would lead to more infections.

By late June, all states had started reopening. Many businesses were allowed to reopen, but they had to follow special rules. These rules included social distancing and extra cleaning. Still, some places remained closed, and many people kept working from home.

Some states, including California, saw increased cases as they reopened.

Health experts said the more time people could spend distancing, the better. Some scientists said the most effective social distancing for the pandemic would last more than a year. They hoped this time would allow researchers to develop a vaccine. Social distancing would keep the number of COVID-19 cases low until people could receive the vaccine. However, these same researchers recognized that rules for distancing would be difficult to enforce.

FURTHER EVIDENCE

Chapter Three has information about social distancing and staying at home. What is the main point of this chapter? What key evidence supports this point? Watch the video about distancing at the website below. Find a quote from the video that supports the chapter's main point.

WHAT IS PHYSICAL DISTANCING?

abdocorelibrary.com/flattening-the-curve

STAYING MENTALLY HEALTHY

COVID-19 changed many parts of people's lives. People felt a lot of different emotions. A pandemic can worsen existing mental health challenges such as depression and anxiety. Experts wanted people to know that it was okay to feel anxious, frustrated, sad, and angry. It was important for people to take steps to stay mentally well.

BIG CHANGES

Changes in people's lives can cause them to feel stressed. COVID-19 changed many

Medical workers were among the many people stressed and saddened by the pandemic.

WHAT IS COLLECTIVE TRAUMA?

Trauma is an emotional response to a life-changing event such as a natural disaster. A pandemic can be considered a traumatic event. COVID-19 changed people's lives. Trauma specialists call the response to large-scale events such as pandemics *collective trauma*. This is when the same traumatic event affects a group of people. The COVID-19 pandemic affected billions of people around the world. Each person copes with trauma differently. Some people seek help from therapists. Some use simple calming methods. One method is to focus on the five senses to calm feelings of stress.

people's routines. Some people lost jobs. Others had to begin working from home. Kids had to complete their school assignments online.

Many people could not visit friends or family while social distancing. Additionally, people did not know when the pandemic would end. People could not make plans for the future. Many worried about what would happen if their family members got sick or if they got sick themselves. Uncertainty can cause feelings of anxiety.

ANXIETY AND DEPRESSION

Two common mental health conditions affected by the pandemic were anxiety and depression. Mental health conditions look different for each person. But there are common symptoms. Anxiety and depression are different from feeling stressed or sad. People often struggle with mental health conditions their entire lives. Some need to see a therapist or take medication.

Anxiety may cause people to feel tired or worried. They may become easily upset. Some people have trouble sleeping or concentrating. They may feel their heart racing. Anxiety makes it hard for people to relax.

Like anxiety, depression looks different for each person. Depression often causes people to feel hopeless or helpless. They may lose interest in hobbies they used to enjoy. Depression may also cause people to have trouble sleeping, or they may sleep too much. People with depression may have trouble making decisions. They may also change their eating habits.

Being alone while social distancing could worsen feelings of depression and anxiety. Many people with mental health conditions coped by staying in contact with friends and family. People often had to find new ways to cope during the pandemic. Some sewed masks for family members and health-care workers. Others took walks outside. Some took more naps. People listened to what their bodies needed. There was no wrong way to cope as long as people stayed safe and healthy.

STAYING WELL

Mental health experts offered several tips to stay mentally well during the pandemic. One was to maintain a schedule. Without school or work, it could be easy to get off a schedule. But experts say waking up at the same time each day helps people feel less stressed. Routines also include eating meals at certain times.

Experts also told people to eat healthfully, get enough sleep, and stay active. These things keep the

Some people coped with the pandemic by staying active.

body balanced. Bodies need nutritious food to have enough energy. Sleep allows bodies to recharge. Exercise releases chemicals in the brain that make people feel happy.

Experts also told people to stay in touch with others. This was still possible while social distancing. People could call or video chat with friends and family. People need to talk to others to be healthy.

HOW DOES FOOD IMPROVE MOOD?

Foods high in sugar and fat cause the brain to release feel-good chemicals. But these feelings do not last. Experts said it was important for people to eat a balanced diet during the pandemic. Many studies show nutrition and mood are linked. A 2019 study from Macquarie University in Australia found that people who ate more fruits and vegetables saw improvement in their depression symptoms. "We need to talk to mental health patients about what they eat," says Drew Ramsey, a psychiatrist at Columbia University in New York. "When people make efforts to care for themselves . . . their mental health is going to improve."

Flattening the curve meant every person had to do his or her part. Washing hands and social distancing helped ensure hospitals did not become overwhelmed. During all these changes, feelings of stress or sadness were common. People could support each other during the pandemic. When people support one another, feelings of loneliness and stress can decrease.

STRAIGHT TO THE
SOURCE

Joshua Gordon was the director of the National Institute of Mental Health during the pandemic. In a letter to the citizens of the United States, Gordon talked about how to cope with negative feelings during the pandemic:

> *Feelings of anxiety and uncertainty are completely normal during times like this. . . . Reach out to friends and family for support, virtually if necessary. . . . It is important to realize that social distancing does not have to mean social isolation, especially with modern technologies available to many of us. Connecting with our friends and loved ones, whether by high-tech means or through simple phone calls, can help us maintain ties during stressful days ahead.*

> Source: Joshua Gordon. "Coping with Coronavirus: Managing Stress, Fear, and Anxiety." *NIMH*, 16 Mar. 2020, nimh.nih.gov. Accessed 28 Apr. 2020.

BACK IT UP

The author of this passage is using evidence to support a point. Write a paragraph describing the point the author is making. Then write down two or three pieces of evidence the author uses to make the point.

FAST FACTS

- COVID-19 is the disease caused by a new coronavirus called SARS-CoV-2.

- The virus can spread through the air and on surfaces.

- The term *curve* describes the rate at which people become infected by a disease.

- Flattening the curve during a pandemic allows hospitals to have enough doctors and equipment to care for all people who become sick.

- Washing with soap and water is the best way to disinfect hands.

- Social distancing limits how many people may come into contact with an infected person.

- The CDC recommended every person wear a cloth face mask to prevent the spread of COVID-19.

- Many people faced increased anxiety and depression during the pandemic due to a change in routines as well as uncertainty about the future.

- Eating well, exercising, and getting enough sleep are important to staying physically and mentally healthy during a pandemic.

Why Do I Care?

Maybe you do not know anyone who became sick from COVID-19. But that doesn't mean you can't think about how to keep other people safe. Do you have friends or family that have pre-existing medical conditions? How might their experience have been different than that of someone without a pre-existing illness during the COVID-19 pandemic?

Another View

This book talks about flattening the curve. As you know, every source is different. Ask a librarian or another adult to help you find another source about this topic. Write a short essay comparing and contrasting the new source's point of view with that of this book's author. What is the point of view of each author? How are they similar and why? How are they different and why?

You Are There

This book discusses how people could stay mentally healthy during the COVID-19 pandemic. Imagine you must stay at home. Write a blog post about what things you'll do to take care of yourself. Be sure to add plenty of detail to your notes.

Take a Stand

Some people think they should not have to wear a mask during a pandemic if they do not want to. Other people believe it is better to wear a mask because it protects other people. Do you think people should be required to wear a mask during a pandemic even if they do not want to? Why or why not?

GLOSSARY

bacteria
organisms that can
sometimes cause disease

droplet
a tiny drop of liquid
or moisture

hygiene
cleanliness, especially in
relation to good health

precaution
a step taken in an attempt to
prevent something

respirator
a mask or device worn over
the mouth and nose that
cleans the air breathed in

respiratory
having to do with the lungs
and airways

symptom
a sign of an illness or other
health condition

therapist
a person trained to help
people cope with mental
illness or trauma

ventilator
a medical machine that helps
people breathe

ONLINE RESOURCES

To learn more about flattening the curve, visit our free resource websites below.

Visit **abdocorelibrary.com** or scan this QR code for free Common Core resources for teachers and students, including vetted activities, multimedia, and booklinks, for deeper subject comprehension.

Visit **abdobooklinks.com** or scan this QR code for free additional online weblinks for further learning. These links are routinely monitored and updated to provide the most current information available.

LEARN MORE

Hustad, Douglas. *Understanding COVID-19*. Abdo Publishing, 2021.

Reinke, Beth Bence. *Nutrition Basics*. Abdo Publishing, 2016.

INDEX

About the Author

Martha London is a writer and educator. She lives in Minnesota with her cat.